OUR FAVORITE BRANDS

STAR WARS

By Martha London

Kaleidoscope
Minneapolis, MN

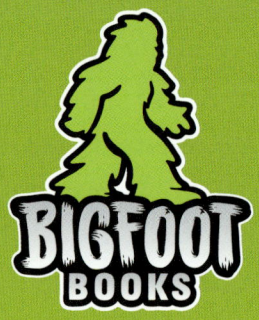

The Quest for Discovery Never Ends

....

This edition is co-published by agreement between Kaleidoscope and World Book, Inc.

Kaleidoscope Publishing, Inc.
6012 Blue Circle Drive
Minnetonka, MN 55343 U.S.A.

World Book, Inc.
180 North LaSalle St., Suite 900
Chicago IL 60601 U.S.A.

All rights reserved. No part of this book may be reproduced in any form without written permission from the publishers.

Kaleidoscope ISBNs
978-1-64519-021-9 (library bound)
978-1-64494-186-7 (paperback)
978-1-64519-121-6 (ebook)

World Book ISBN
978-0-7166-4321-0 (library bound)

Library of Congress Control Number
2019939234

Text copyright ©2020 by Kaleidoscope Publishing, Inc. All-Star Sports, Bigfoot Books, and associated logos are trademarks and/or registered trademarks of Kaleidoscope Publishing, Inc.

Printed in the United States of America.

FIND ME IF YOU CAN!

Bigfoot lurks within one of the images in this book. It's up to you to find him!

TABLE OF CONTENTS

Chapter 1: The Last Jedi 4

Chapter 2: Making a Universe 10

Chapter 3: May the Force Be with You 16

Chapter 4: A Worldwide Craze 22

    Beyond the Book 28
    Research Ninja 29
    Further Resources 30
    Glossary 31
    Index 32
    Photo Credits 32
    About the Author 32

CHAPTER 1

Fans of all ages eagerly wait for new *Star Wars* movies to come out.

The Last Jedi

Sara walks into the theater. She has her popcorn and soda. The theater is pretty full. There are people of all ages. Teenagers sit in the back. Older people sit on the sides. The first *Star Wars* movie came out in 1977. Sara thinks they probably saw it in theaters back then.

Sara finds a seat in the middle. She wants to see the whole screen. Sara has been waiting for months. She can't wait to see *The Last Jedi*.

Soon, the lights dim. Sara scoots down in her seat. Her soda is in the cup holder. The popcorn sits on her lap. The screen goes black.

Then the music starts. Trumpets play. Sara would know the *Star Wars* theme anywhere. The **iconic** text appears. It starts, "A long time ago in a galaxy far, far away…"

The two and a half hours fly by. The credits roll. Sara sighs. She loved the film. Sara has seen all of the *Star Wars* movies. She loves space travel. Someday, she thinks people will walk on Mars.

The Last Jedi *premiered in 2017.*

For Sara, *Star Wars* is more than just movies. It's a huge part of her life. Last year, Sara dressed up as Princess Leia Organa for Halloween. She is excited to see more movies.

Disney built a large model of the Star Wars *theme park to give fans a preview.*

Sara's family is planning a trip to Disney World. There's a new *Star Wars* theme park there. She can't wait to ride in the Millennium Falcon. She and her family will meet Chewbacca. Together, they'll wander the streets of strange planets.

FUN FACT
An early version of *The Force Awakens* was titled *Shadow of the Empire.*

CHAPTER 2

Making a Universe

George Lucas sat in his apartment. He thought about comics he read as a kid. Lucas loved stories about space. He wanted to make a movie. But first, he needed a **script**. He had many ideas. He imagined Luke Skywalker as an old general. Han Solo was a green alien.

He called his project *Star Wars*. Lucas asked **producers** to help pay for the movie. Many companies turned him down. But 20th Century Fox gave Lucas a chance. He could keep working.

The story was long. It was confusing. No one could follow it. Lucas had to rethink his story. He went back to the beginning. What did he want this movie to be? He wanted it to be an adventure. But he also wanted the movie to be different. He didn't want *Star Wars* to look like other science fiction movies. He rewrote the script many times. It took him two years to finish.

George Lucas is a director and writer best known for creating the Star Wars *universe*.

A CHANGE OF SCENERY

Science fiction movies before *Star Wars* were shiny. The planets were clean. Ships were sleek. People wore tight clothes. George Lucas wanted his world to look like people lived in it. *Star Wars* was dirty. There was dust everywhere. Han Solo's ship was falling apart. People liked this new look.

Because their budget was small, Lucas and the movie's cast and crew could only do a few takes of each scene before they had to move on.

Lucas took the script to 20th Century Fox. He knew that the movie was going to be expensive. The film took place on different planets. Some parts took place on spaceships. That wasn't going to be cheap. But the **budget** he got was small. The team had only $11 million to work with. This meant they were low on supplies like **film**. Each scene only got a few **takes**. Then they had to move on.

The crew filmed in different places. One place was a desert in northern Africa. Orange sand stretched as far as the eye could see. The sky was a bright blue. It was the perfect location to create the dry planet Tatooine.

FUN FACT
It only took two and a half hours to record Darth Vader's lines.

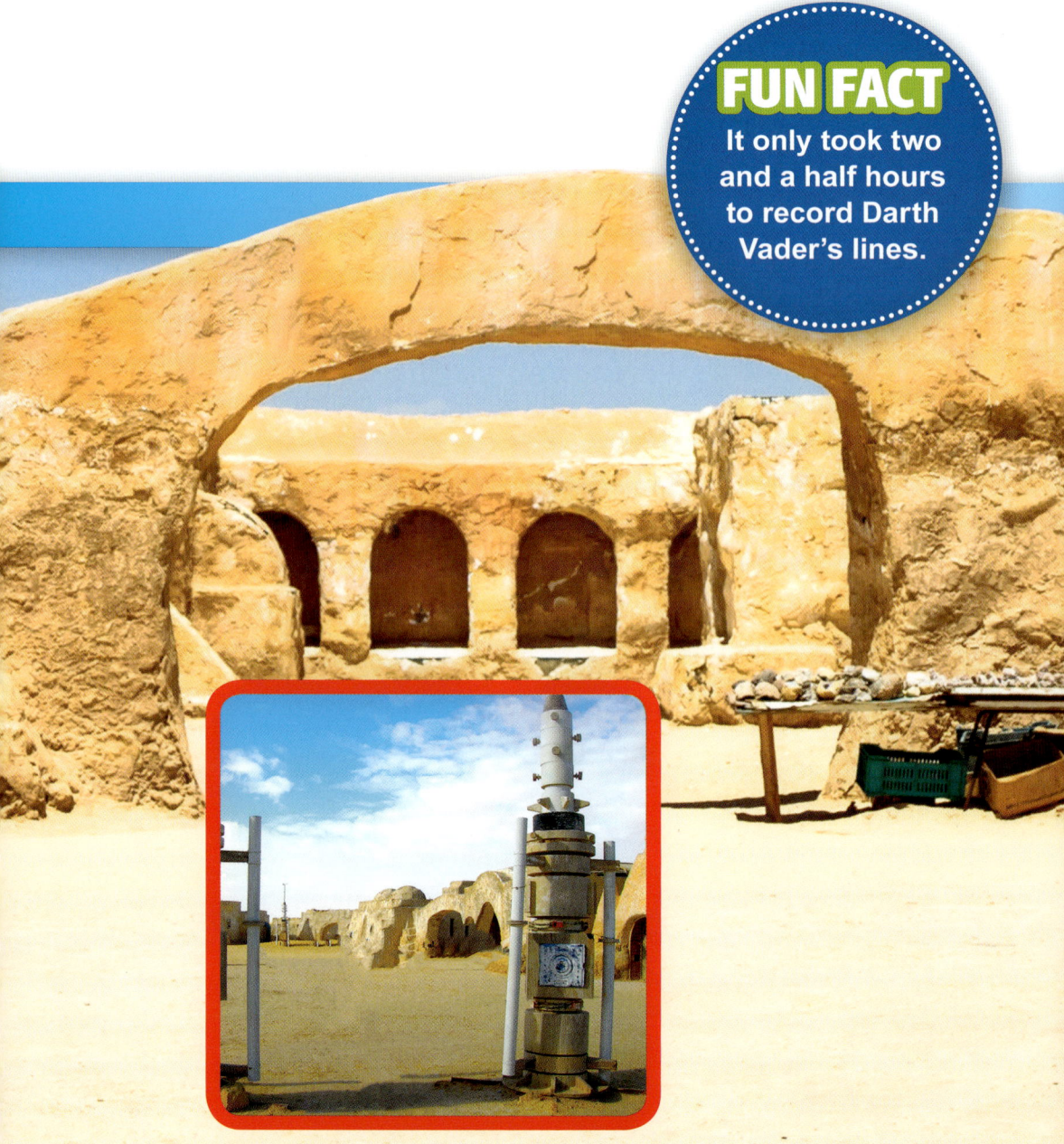

Star Wars came out in 1977. It made a lot of money. Many people saw the film. It was a new kind of science fiction. George Lucas had created a universe. Now he wanted to build an empire.

Some of Star Wars was filmed in an African desert to create the planet Tatooine.

CHAPTER 3

May the Force Be with You

George Lucas knew what to do next. He found a new adventure for his characters. *Star Wars* became a **franchise**. The first movie was renamed *A New Hope*. This way other movies could also be called *Star Wars*. *Star Wars* was a hit. Some kids battled with plastic light sabers. They made the sound effects from the movies. Others enjoyed books, games, and more.

A New Hope made *Star Wars* popular. Lucas started working on the next one. But producers wouldn't give him enough money. Lucas ran out of money while making the second movie. But the toys were still selling. Toy sales paid for film costs.

Star Wars *inspired many new products, such as the* Star Wars: The Clone Wars *version of Monopoly.*

CARRIE FISHER

Carrie Fisher played Leia in the *Star Wars* films. In the first three films, Leia is a princess. In the later movies, Leia is older. She is a general. Fisher spoke out about mental illness. People admired her for being a mental health advocate.

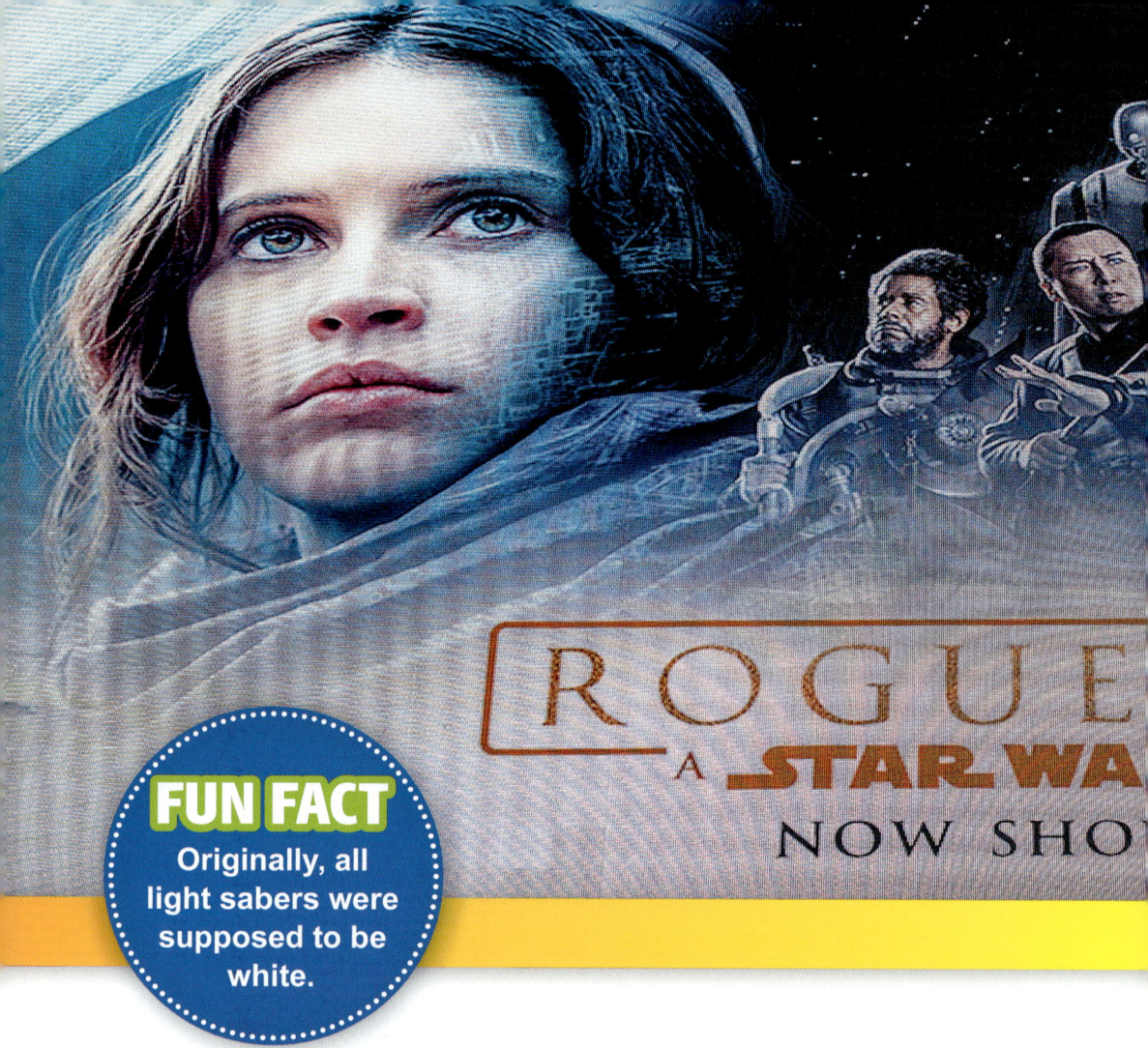

FUN FACT
Originally, all light sabers were supposed to be white.

Recently, Lucas sold his company, Lucasfilm. Disney bought it in 2012. Disney saw more stories in the *Star Wars* universe. It started making new movies. People got excited about *Star Wars* again.

New episodes in the series started coming out in 2015. Movies like *Rogue One* and *Solo* were also released. Millions of people rushed to theaters to see them.

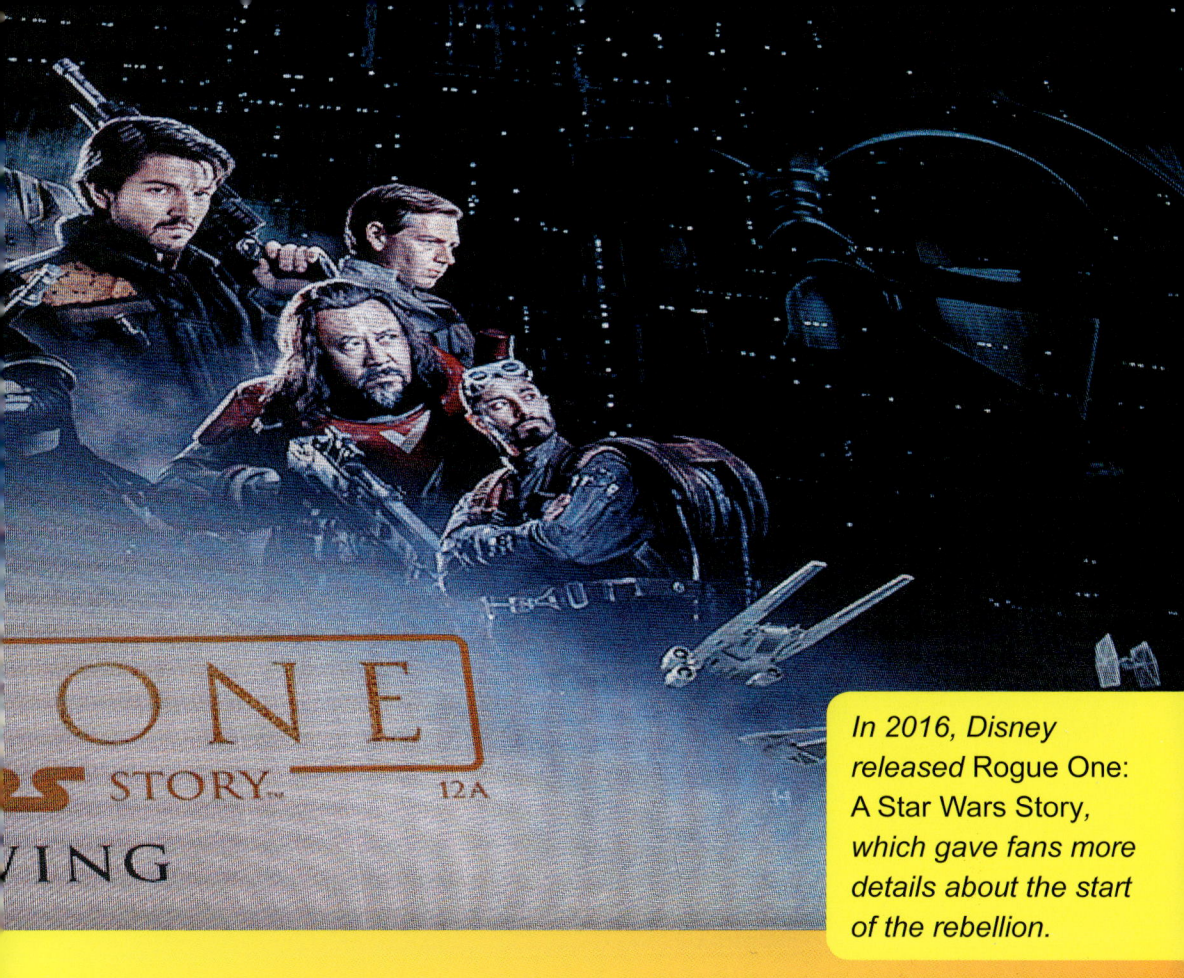

In 2016, Disney released Rogue One: A Star Wars Story, which gave fans more details about the start of the rebellion.

People were excited to learn more about *Star Wars*. Fans saw what happened after *Episode VI*. They met the characters who started the fight against the Empire. They saw Han Solo as a young man.

Disney had another idea. It wanted to bring *Star Wars* to Earth. Disney began building *Star Wars* theme parks. Visitors can explore the planets and ships in person. Chewbacca walks around the park. Guests travel to new worlds. The lights dim. Music plays over speakers.

STAR WARS TIMELINE

**1983
Episode VI:
Return of the Jedi**

**1977
Episode IV:
A New Hope
is released in
theaters under
the title
Star Wars.**

1977   1980   1983   1989   1992   1995   1998

**1980
Episode V:
The Empire
Strikes Back**

**1999
Episode I:
The Phantom
Menace**

LEGO releases its first *Star Wars* set.

2002
Episode II:
Attack of the
Clones

2008
The Clone Wars

2019
Episode IX:
The Rise of
Skywalker

2017
Episode VIII:
The Last Jedi

2015
Episode VII:
The Force
Awakens

2001 2004 2007 2010 2013 2016 2019

2005
Episode III:
Revenge of
the Sith

2016
Rogue One:
A Star Wars
Story

2012
Disney buys
Lucasfilm and
Star Wars for
$4 billion.

2018
Solo: A Star
Wars Story

21

CHAPTER 4

Star Wars *and its sequels were some of the first summer blockbuster movies.*

FUN FACT
Star Wars was dubbed in Navajo.

A Worldwide Craze

A New Hope came to theaters in 1977. The idea of a summer blockbuster was new. Before that, summer movies were not very popular. People played outside. They jumped in pools and relaxed in the sun. Movie companies didn't think summer movies could be hits.

A New Hope helped change that. It became one of the highest-**grossing** films ever. Companies learned that they could release movies over the summer. A summer movie could be a big hit. *A New Hope* became popular around the world. Luke, Han, and Leia are known across the globe. The movie was popular with people of all ages.

BOX OFFICE SALES

Episode IV: A New Hope — $1.26 billion

Episode VII: The Force Awakens — $954 million

Episode I: The Phantom Menace — $749 million

Episode VI: Return of the Jedi — $715 million

Episode V: The Empire Strikes Back — $696 million

Episode VIII: The Last Jedi — $596 million

Rogue One: A Star Wars Story — $533 million

Episode III: Revenge of the Sith — $523 million

Episode II: Attack of the Clones — $459 million

Solo: A Star Wars Story — $201 million

Scientists are inspired by Star Wars *to develop new technology like bionic hands and arms.*

Expensive movies came out before *A New Hope*. But they were usually for adults. *Star Wars* was different. Adults enjoyed the movies, but they were made for teenagers.

But *Star Wars* didn't only change movies. It also inspired scientists. They made devices like ones in *Star Wars*. Their inventions help people around the world. They help kids like Ellie. She has a **bionic** hand like Luke Skywalker's.

Kids around the world play with Star Wars *action figures*, read Star Wars *books*, and dress as their favorite characters.

Ellie loves *Star Wars*. She watched all the movies with her dad. Luke's bionic hand moved easily. Ellie's is green. When she puts it on, she can move all the fingers. Ellie picks up a cup of water. She can't usually do that on her own.

Star Wars is here to stay. New films, toys, and theme parks keep the story going. People around the world will enjoy *Star Wars* for years to come.

BEYOND
THE BOOK

After reading the book, it's time to think about what you learned. Try the following exercises to jumpstart your ideas.

THINK

DIFFERENT SOURCES. What other types of sources could you use to learn about *Star Wars*? How might each source be useful in its own way?

CREATE

PRIMARY SOURCES. Primary sources are pieces of information that haven't been filtered through another source. Interviews with directors, scripts, and unused movie film are all examples of primary sources. Make a list of some possible primary sources you could use to learn more about *Star Wars*.

SHARE

SUM IT UP. Write a paragraph that summarizes the important information from this book. Remember to write the paragraph in your own words. Don't just copy the words in the book. Share your summary with a classmate. Does your classmate have any feedback about the summary or questions you might be able to answer?

GROW

DRAWING CONNECTIONS. How do you think *Star Wars* relates to space exploration? How does learning about space help you understand *Star Wars*? Make a Venn diagram to show the connections and differences between the two topics.

RESEARCH NINJA

Visit **www.ninjaresearcher.com/0219** to learn how to take your research skills and book report writing to the next level!

RESEARCH

DIGITAL LITERACY TOOLS

SEARCH LIKE A PRO
Learn about how to use search engines to find useful websites.

FACT OR FAKE?
Discover how you can tell a trusted website from an untrustworthy resource.

TEXT DETECTIVE
Explore how to zero in on the information you need most.

SHOW YOUR WORK
Research responsibly—learn how to cite sources.

WRITE

GET TO THE POINT
Learn how to express your main ideas.

PLAN OF ATTACK
Learn prewriting exercises and create an outline.

DOWNLOADABLE REPORT FORMS

Further Resources

BOOKS

Betts, Bruce, PhD. *Astronomy for Kids*. Rockridge Press, 2018.

Hidalgo, Pablo, and Simon Beecroft. *Star Wars Character Encyclopedia*. DK, 2016.

Sumerak, Marc. *Star Wars: Droidography*. Harper Festival, 2018.

WEBSITES

Factsurfer.com gives you a safe, fun way to find more information.

1. Go to www.factsurfer.com.
2. Enter "Star Wars" into the search box and click 🔍.
3. Select your book cover to see a list of related websites.

Glossary

advocate: An advocate is a person who talks about issues in order to help other people. Carrie Fisher was a mental health advocate.

bionic: A bionic device is a machine that replaces any part of the human body. Luke Skywalker got a bionic hand.

budget: A budget is the amount of money that a company is allowed to use for a project. The budget for the first *Star Wars* movie was $11 million.

film: Film is the plastic material that movies are recorded on. It is used less commonly today. George Lucas didn't receive much money for supplies like film.

franchise: A franchise is a group of movies or other products about the same characters or universe. Disneyland's Galaxy's Edge theme park is part of the *Star Wars* franchise.

grossing: Grossing is making a total amount of money. The *Star Wars* movies are some of the highest-grossing films ever.

iconic: Iconic means easy to recognize. Yoda is an iconic character in the *Star Wars* movies.

producers: Producers are people who give money for movies to be made. Lucas asked producers to help him make *Star Wars*.

script: A script is the written lines that actors say in a movie. The script for *Star Wars* took two years to finish.

takes: Takes are different recordings of the same scene. The *Star Wars* cast and crew could only do a few takes of each scene.

Index

20th Century Fox, 10, 13

Chewbacca, 9, 16, 19

Disney, 9, 18–19, 21

Fisher, Carrie, 17
Force Awakens, The, 9, 21, 24

Last Jedi, The, 5–6, 21, 24
Lucas, George, 10, 12, 13, 15, 16, 18
Lucasfilm, 18, 21

New Hope, A, 5, 12, 13–15, 16, 20, 23, 24, 25

Organa, Leia, 8, 17, 23

Rogue One, 18–19, 21, 24

Skywalker, Luke, 10, 23, 25, 27
Solo, 18–19, 21, 24
Solo, Han, 10, 12, 19, 23
spaceships, 9, 12, 13, 19

theme parks, 9, 19, 27
toys, 16, 20, 27

PHOTO CREDITS

The images in this book are reproduced through the courtesy of: Brendan Hunter/iStockphoto, front cover (Millennium Falcon); Stefano Buttafoco/Shutterstock Images, front cover (Darth Vader); Sergey Klopotov/Shutterstock Images, front cover (R2-D2); Andrea Raffin/Shutterstock Images, front cover (Chewbacca); suns07butterfly/Shutterstock Images, front cover (stars); Roberto Galan/Shutterstock Images, 2, 21 (top left); Zoriana Zaitseva/Shutterstock Images, 4–5; Jeff Bukowski/Shutterstock Images, 5; Willrow Hood/Shutterstock Images, 6, 20 (top); Sarunyu L/Shutterstock Images, 6–7, 21 (top right); Jeff Gritchen/Orange County Register/Getty Images, 8–9; Denis Makarenko/Shutterstock Images, 11; Sunset Boulevard/Corbis/Corbis Historical/Getty Images, 12–13; Solarisys/Shutterstock Images, 14; Lukasz Janyst/Shutterstock Images, 14–15; TracyHornbrook/iStockphoto, 16–17; Kathy Hutchins/Shutterstock Images, 17; John Gomez/Shutterstock Images, 18–19; Ekaterina_Minaeva/Shutterstock Images, 20 (middle); Yuri Turkov/Shutterstock Images, 20 (bottom); Stefano Buttafoco/Shutterstock Images, 21 (bottom), 30; George Widman/AP Images, 22–23; Tanupong Wittayanukullak/Shutterstock Images, 24 (popcorn); Danila2332/Shutterstock Images, 25; Chekyravaa/Shutterstock Images, 26–27; Bakounine/Shutterstock Images, 27.

ABOUT THE AUTHOR

Martha London is a writer from Minnesota. She grew up watching all of the *Star Wars* movies. Martha lives in the Twin Cities.